THE BOOK OF POEMS AND
CONVERSATIONAL TRIGGERS

LLEWELLYN GEORGE

Order this book online at www.trafford.com
or email orders@trafford.com

Most Trafford titles are also available at major online book retailers.

Printed in the United States of America.

ISBN: 978-1-4669-3806-9 (sc)
ISBN: 978-1-4669-3805-2 (hc)
ISBN: 978-1-4669-3804-5 (e)

Library of Congress Control Number: 2012909826

Trafford rev. 05/31/2012

www.trafford.com

North America & International
toll-free: 1 888 232 4444 (USA & Canada)
phone: 250 383 6864 ♦ fax: 812 355 4082

CONTENTS

Grateful acknowledgment is made to

Chanel George
Yannick George
Sharon Waller
Brenda Roberts

Special Acknowledgment

This book is dedicated to
My wonderful mother

Marjorie C. George
For the guidance that directed
Me through the many obstacles of life.
You are very special!
I thank God for you, Mom!

Love, Llewellyn

Conversational Triggers are the spoken words
that are used to strike a conversation.

WHO I AM

There is a man from a sacred land
An island that sits in the sun
He lives his life to the fullest he can
Laughing and joking, he always walks around
With nothing on his mind
But the extension of a helping hand
Day in and day out, I could hear him shout
The sound of laughter and joy
Always comes from his mouth
There's hardly a time I ever see him pout
In his life, there's always days and no nights
Now that you have read of me
I must reveal to you
I am who I am, and all I want to be is who I am
So please, enjoy the spoken words that I speak!

AFTER TODAY

As the history of my life engulfs and arouses my memory
Some thoughts of the past I must let be
With serenity in mind to the mountain I make my climb
Repulsive I shall be to the rushing wave of misery
Without apprehension, a new day I'll embrace under the sun
Tomorrow, tomorrow please come free of sorrow
Yesterday has taken me places that I never knew
So please tomorrow, take me places I would like to go
On my face, the glow of your light will be reflected
Clearly I'll see the path to where I make my journey
In the tune of yesterday, absent was the melody of the sparrow
Tomorrow, tomorrow I see you coming over the horizon
Into the day after today, I'll fly on your golden wings
And to me, I hope joy and happiness you will bring.

CONVERSATIONAL TRIGGERS

1. Hello, is everything well?
2. You make that dress look so beautiful!
3. Hello, can you please tell me the time?
4. Did you hear the weekend forecast?
5. Do you think that politicians are a little selfish?
6. Nice choice of color for the occasion.
7. Hmm, the smell of food is in the air.
8. I love this kind of temperature.
9. Hi, what's the name of that tree?
10. May I assist you?

FLOWERS

I am the stem and you are the rose
The garden is a place for us to grow
How well we will grow no one knows
We were planted with lots of hope
That by chance we may be strong
Instead of just standing tall
We could be both if we want to be
Flowers are like lovers, so the garden says
They stay together from day to day
Even if the sun or rain stays away
Sharing the same bed in our life
Feeling each other's roots in the night
Oh, honey, it's such a beautiful sight
Flowers are like lovers, so the garden says
So please don't let anyone get in our way
And most of all, don't let them take you away
Flowers are like lovers, so the garden says.

CONVERSATIONAL TRIGGERS

1. Look at that over there!
2. Sir, what's your opinion on the latest in Washington?
3. That blue dress is as pretty as the sky.
4. The days are getting shorter; winter is coming.
5. Well, well, are you going into the water?
6. Good day, can you tell me where your accent is from?
7. The hometown team won yesterday.
8. Hello, is there a train delay?
9. Did you hear of that tragedy?
10. You have a very soothing smile.

TALKING HANDS

If you coat your belly with the fruits of love
Easy it will be to digest the feelings of others
So remove some thoughts from self and unto your fellowmen
Follow the guiding light to the place in which they stand
Now, reflect the glow of your welcoming eyes
Like a magnet, to the hands of others your hand will be attracted
Let it be known that a greeting is done by an outstretched hand
Wait not for the hands of other to commute
With a hand extended, by what is reciprocated you'll be rewarded
Like a printed scroll, it should be read and understood
Hands that stay apart will never meet.

CONVERSATIONAL TRIGGERS

1. The bus is extremely late!
2. The hometown team won last night.
3. Did you see that new movie?
4. Isn't it very peaceful around here?
5. Thank you, you are so considerate.
6. Spring is in the air.
7. Very handsome son!
8. Can you eat on the train?
9. What is the name of the number one song?
10. You have beautiful long legs. Are you a dancer?

MY FIRST LADY

Hi, Mom! Job well done I must say
Strong and tall in your past days, you once stood
Which encouraged me to be the best that I could
As a body of one, your possession of wisdom is that of many
Always willing to share with those you know and many more
In the oven of your mind, the bread of wisdom was baked
And given to those who had less and the hungry, like me
So that I may swim in the sea of knowledge effortlessly
Arriving at many ports that I've never seen
Spreading the word of wisdom has always been my dream
Hi, Mom! I must say, the able in you has gone away
And never to return for the rest of your days
But the knowledge you shared
Has changed people in so many ways
Hi, Mom! Job well done, I must say.

CONVERSATIONAL TRIGGERS

1. Such a beautiful girl!
2. These trains are kept very clean.
3. That rain was badly needed.
4. There are so many police cars in the area, what's up?
5. Good morning, you're dressed so professional.
6. How long were you waiting on your flight?
7. Security around here is awfully tight.
8. Do you feel a little nervous being in banks?
9. Thank God, we were spared from the storm!
10. Hello, is this the best time of the month for planting?

OUR CASTLE

The beauty of the physical body is obvious to see
To penetrate the walls of the inner beauty is most intriguing to me
As we communicate in the medium of soft-spoken words
The energy of continuity will be established by the look in our
eager eyes
Like an open window, our minds will welcome our words of thoughts
The meaning of what is said, will be reflective of who we are
And with the substance of our minds, we'll dine
With the strength of our union, our building needs will be gathered
By the company of trust, our castle of love will be built
With a double portion of spirituality, our castle will be blessed
As one, our business of love, we will manage
And with the profit, one day we'll renew our vows.

CONVERSATIONAL TRIGGERS

1. Thanks for trains, no more traffic delays.
2. Did you see the devastation caused by the storm?
3. What is the shortest distance between two points?
4. Hi, sir, how long have you been in the military?
5. What a wonderful child!
6. Have you ever been to the islands?
7. Can you swim?
8. Did you look at the big fight last night?
9. Who is your favorite singer?
10. That was a pretty horse that won the Kentucky Derby.

FULFILLMENT

Seek the light and enjoy the fruits of life
View your life not as a rehearsal
Time is of essence, so fulfill your dreams
OK, it is to dream of the outrageous
Which may seem distant to the visually impaired
Remove self from the grips of darkness
Seek the light and enjoy the fruits of life
Be wise, open your eyes, and take command
Am I someone of substance or just an existence, I must ask
The positive revelation led to my confirmation
That the someone in me has risen like a pinnacle
To be seen and heard even by the visually impaired.

CONVERSATIONAL TRIGGERS

1. What races determine the Triple Crown?
2. Thanks for serving your country!
3. Who is your favorite actor?
4. What is the nearest planet to earth?
5. Can I tell you that you are beautiful?
6. Did you see that beautiful moon last night?
7. Who won the last heavyweight title fight?
8. I love the color of your tie.
9. You look very nice in pinstripe.
10. What was the number one movie this weekend?

TWO HEARTS ONE LOVE

Like diamonds, our anniversaries are forever
They just keep on coming and coming
And our roots of love will keep on growing
As a tower, our love can be seen from afar
Peeking above the hills under the open sky
With the inscription that says,
"Together as one, we are forever."
With the fuel of trust and understanding
Our engine of love will keep on running
Not to be slowed even for a moment in time
The synchronized beats of our hearts
Will be heard as a sound of one
To the love of each other, we surrender
And the loving days spent together
We'll never forget to remember.

CONVERSATIONAL TRIGGERS

1. That is a very distinguished mustache.
2. Did you get your good looks from Mom or Dad?
3. What is your Alma Mater?
4. Isn't it beautiful seeing the birds fly?
5. Did you see the dog show the other day?
6. I see that you are very athletic.
7. Very interesting shoes!
8. I am going on a cruise. Have you ever been on one?
9. What's your vacation plans?
10. Are you happy that the children are back in school?

ADMIRATION OF A FATHER

As I scan the pictures in my mind
A wave of reminiscence rush upon me
Your contribution of love and care in my life
Has yielded someone special in the like of me
And of you, special is all that I've ever seen
By the penetrating tone of your composed voice
The deliverance of transforming qualities I receive
That was absorbed by my receptive ears
And the wall of objection was demolished
In the presence of my open eyes
Easier it became to see the front line of life
Which for many, may be very far and out of sight
And thanks I'll say to you
For the shoulder of wisdom that carry me through
And forever in my hall of fame, you'll be enshrined.

CONVERSATIONAL TRIGGERS

1. The work of God is amazing.
2. What grade is your son in?
3. Do you think there is a need for better schools?
4. I hope that the bus is not crowded.
5. Beautiful hat! Who is it made by?
6. Very nice car! What's the year?
7. Where is the closest hospital?
8. I love to admire a beautiful woman driving a truck.
9. You are such a lady!
10. Did you see the spelling bee?

LIGHT

The extreme velocity of your travel
Will always be attempted by the curious minds of man
From afar, to distant eyes you radiate rapidly
In the universal jungle, you are like a lion on land
The living thrives when you are present
But could die if you are too intense
In your presence at the peak of day
Some find it difficult to stay
But of the plants, you are received throughout the day
At times it seems that they wish you would go away
When the cycle of day ends, leaves look rejuvenated again
Into the night, your many substitutes comes to sight
Which can separate the honest from the dishonest ones
Before I retire at night, I never forget to put you out
As the day breaks, happy again I will be to see you radiate.

CONVERSATIONAL TRIGGERS

1. Why is the wait so long to see a doctor?
2. What is your favorite food?
3. Can lightning strike the same place twice?
4. What would you say was the most important invention?
5. Hello, miss, can you tell me the date of the month?
6. Doesn't it seem as if the weekend flies?
7. Hi, sir, where is the Pentagon located?
8. Bless you for being so concerned for humanity.
9. Hmm, it's extra hot today.
10. Women have really come a long way.

LOVE REFLECTION

As the stream of wind shapes your curls into strands of hair
The beauty of nature can be seen by the eyes of every man
Stare now into the mirror of the wonderful world
Can you see the "all" that I've always seen?
The wonder of all women with eyes of magnetic force
Just hold my hand, and I'll direct you to the land in which we seek
The tallest peak of a picturesque beach we'll claim
With your hands of satin
The glitter can be touched in the knee-high sand
With your magnetic eyes
The water will be attracted for clear viewing
Oh, honey, the mermaids are there—can you see?
No, the reflection you see is of you and me
And forever in love we'll always be.

CONVERSATIONAL TRIGGERS

1. Why is the wait so long to see a dentist?
2. The mind of a scientist is exceptional.
3. Why do some psychiatrists look strange?
4. Does it seem like months are as short as weeks?
5. What is your favorite snack?
6. Water is my favorite drink. What's yours?
7. Sir, who is the fastest runner in the world?
8. I bet that car runs very well.
9. Was your dad in the military?
10. Look at the steam coming from the street as the rain falls.

DAUGHTER OF LIFE

Now that the foundation of life has been erected
Your palace of maturity will be constructed
Attention must be paid to the material of which it is built
By the strength of the structure, the material's quality will be
evident
Your choice of builders should be of a class that's second to none
With cut back nails and anxious hands, commence your project
of life
Take notice of the treacherous terrain in which your palace stands
Be not afraid of the consuming valleys and roaming hills
As you would with your nails, polish the inner you to perfection
Relax your mind to the pace of a calming wind
And the process of positive decision making will become a breeze.

CONVERSATIONAL TRIGGERS

1. Isn't the space shuttle launch beautiful to watch?
2. Thanks for the seat. How are you doing?
3. Thank goodness it's Friday.
4. What is your opinion on veterans' health care?
5. What is your preference, coffee or tea?
6. Do you save your accumulated change?
7. Why do some plants change color before it rains?
8. Smile and make someone glad.
9. Who is more emotional, man or woman?
10. Is it safe to say that love is most important in life?

BALANCE

Sometimes I'm like a wave at sea
Peaking to the sky and then falling low
Often it's a task to exit my open door
Most days I'm lifted up, but often I feel down
Other days, I have no clue to who I am
The beauty of joy is obscured by my ugly frown
The fighter that I am keeps me from being overrun
To the ripples in my wave, the exit I will expose
And like the calm on the open sea I'll feel
In my life, the results of positivity again I'll see
My appreciation of you the almighty, I will exhibit
By my enhanced performance on life's stage
Blessed am I for the gift of peace that was given.

CONVERSATIONAL TRIGGERS

1. The process of life is so complicated, it amazes me.
2. What if the universe wasn't aligned properly?
3. Does the moon seem to pull you in sometimes?
4. What is the most popular girl's name?
5. Hump day is here, two more days to go.
6. Do you really think that a dog is man's best friend?
7. What is the fastest airplane?
8. Are you computer savvy?
9. Are you concerned with the radiation that cell phones emit?
10. Have you ever gone fishing?

LANGUAGE OF LOVE

Touch me and make me believe
Hold my hand and electrified I'll become
Talk to me, and special I'll feel
Whisper as a soft-spoken flower
The words of love, which last forever
Look into my eyes with your soothing stare
And now generate the excitement that draws me near
Speak softly of you and me
And the tune of silent love you'll sing
Which can be heard by the keenness of my listening ears
Come closer and cover me with your sheet of passion
And let's polish our lips with wetness as we caress.

CONVERSATIONAL TRIGGERS

1. It would be an adventure to ride a horse to the mountains.
2. Do you think that NASCAR drivers are very courageous?
3. How far do you have to travel to get into space?
4. What is the most popular boy's name?
5. What is the fastest cruise ship?
6. When is graduation day?
7. Is your injury healing well?
8. Who won the last college basketball championship?
9. If a dog is man's best friend, what is a cat to a woman?
10. Hi, good looking, are you having fun?

BACK ON TRACK

To you the distance, but redeemable one
Why was your road of travel chosen?
Was it the use of a shortcut you were pursuing?
Or was it a shortened life you were seeking?
Turn back! And let the shadow of doom cast to your rear
Out of the darkened tunnel you'll surface on walking feet
Go on! And stride onto the lighted street of life
Stop now! And on motionless feet
Be attentive to the music that surrounds
The sweet sound is not of which you are accustomed
It's just the drums of opportunity beating all around
Choose the beat with the rhythm of positive notes
At your very best! Go and dance in the hall of success!

CONVERSATIONAL TRIGGERS

1. I thought I saw you at the mall earlier.
2. I am so sorry you got drenched in the rain.
3. In all sports, what team has won the most championships?
4. Did you have a good sleep last night?
5. Hello, dear, you carry your age very well.
6. Oh! You resemble a beautiful rose.
7. Earth colors bring out the purity of your complexion.
8. Do you like landscape scenery or just plain grass?
9. Is the traditional white uniform of nurses obsolete?
10. What a beautiful voice! Are you a singer?

RIVER EYES

Hi, the most beautiful woman under the sun
In the waterway of your eyes to your heart the journey begins
The luggage I carry is filled with love and fruits of passion
As your magnetic eyes guide me closer to the port of entry
A prayer I will say, "Please take me safely to your fountain of love."
As I sail through the still waters of your river eyes
With hands needed not to steer, I felt the soft, still water
And the darkness now creeps upon the sailing surface
Away I am now from the externals that distort the thoughts of
others
By my progression past the sensory city, I am now being taken
The revealed beauty is that of which was expected
Internally, a shower of electrical pulses can be felt
Happy and not afraid, I will now make my descent
In the downward current of your throat, I'll float
To your fountain of love, the direction I will seek
Like a beacon, the romantic beat of your heart I'll use
And by your kindness, I'll be led to the place in which I'll dwell.

CONVERSATIONAL TRIGGERS

1. With all that rain, your hair looks untouched.
2. To you I'll say "Happy Mother's Day" every day!
3. It looks as if you are the happy one in happy father's day.
4. Which cause more devastation, tornadoes or hurricanes?
5. Where is the location of the tallest building in the world?
6. What do you think is the biggest global problem?
7. The gray in your hair is so appealing to my eyes!
8. Do you pay attention to the beauty of the sunset?
9. I never knew that crying was so therapeutic.
10. Why is "bless you" said after someone sneezes?

POSITIVE NOTION

Am I negative because of me?
Or is it due to the depth of my spirituality?
Must I change or should I remain the same?
Into the spiritual garden I must make my entry
The revealed truth to and of me I must now bring
I am a leaf on that tree called humanity
So why shouldn't I display the positive essence of me?
The negative that's within is suppressing my energy of reward
Enjoyable things I'll see under, above, and around
In anguish must I be consumed or triumphant must I be?
With sincerity, the latter of the two I choose
The illumination of the sun will glow and the river of life will flow
Rising up like a budding flower, I'm now ready to let my beauty show
And forever I will float in the tranquil cloud of reward energy.

CONVERSATIONAL TRIGGERS

1. I can't stand to hear anymore about those troublemakers.
2. Is it amazing how colors can change your mood?
3. The other day I saw a black squirrel for the first time.
4. Do you ever wonder how many stars are in the universe?
5. Hello, the smell of your fragrance is very captivating.
6. Have you ever been bird-watching?
7. Those cars are very economical.
8. That suit fits you so well. Are you a tailor?
9. Do you like bike riding?
10. Is the drought really affecting the price of fruits?

JUST FOR YOU

My future love! To you, the sweetness I'll deliver
Like a swarm of excited bees
I'll float your way on open wings
The honey I deliver will be digested by your consuming body
And to me, the sweetest woman you'll become
On your rosy cheeks the look of candy can be seen
With the taste of your candied cheeks
To your sweetness I'll submit
And to your loving and caring ways, I'll gravitate
As I venture into the rooms of your sacred kingdom
The glow of your diamond encrusted crown will diminish
On the reflection of your natural beauty my attention I'll place
The pleasures of your excitement I'll embrace
Now let's wear our bracelets of love for the world to see.

CONVERSATIONAL TRIGGERS

1. Have you noticed that along the shores are always level?
2. Why are there so many shades of blue in the ocean?
3. Have you ever seen the underwater world?
4. I have a question for you: are you a model?
5. Who said gray is of the old? You proved them wrong!
6. Have you ever visited any of the monuments in Washington?
7. Do you like to see the flight pattern of migratory birds?
8. The drought is causing the farmers lots of money.
9. Protect your investment with a wise mind.
10. Stress is a very serious problem in our society.

SON OF MAN

The wheels of tomorrow may never turn
If the gears of today are misaligned
Made by God, the beauty of a masterpiece in you I see
On arrival, the positive that enter must be received
The abundance of distorted thoughts will diminish
In the sea, the wave of uncertainty will remain
With the wind, the obstacles of life will be taken
Wash in the cleansing water of your breathing air
Lubricate with the moisture of your God-given blood
Read your mind and see the informative book it is
Go now, like a fearless soldier and penetrate the wall of life
Like the vibrant colors of a rainbow, life will glow
Now, start your engine and move on!

CONVERSATIONAL TRIGGERS

1. The greed of humanity contributed to a lot of problems.
2. The reckless behavior of some world leaders must stop.
3. Is soccer the number one sport in the world?
4. Does it seem that sunset is the quietest time of day?
5. It's a shame that some people make others miserable.
6. What fruits are rich in vitamin C?
7. You are a true fashion statement.
8. Which is your favorite meal of the day?
9. How many laps have you jogged?
10. What is the distance of this trail?

NATURAL ROMANCE

The thunder of your love
Vibrates the inner walls of my heart
Illuminated by your stroke of lightning
The love you have within is conspicuous to me
Now, strike me with your raindrops
And see me quiver as the chills penetrate within
Refreshed I am now and ready for the journey
Into a world of cheering flowers and dancing roses
Hand in hand, we'll stroll the road of matted grass
Searching for that place most comforting to both
Though impaired by the thick night blanket of dark
Faintly, a vision appeared to me
Oh! It's the city of matrimony
If you may, shall we please now enter?
And to the tune of the whistling wind
We'll dance a love song.

CONVERSATIONAL TRIGGERS

1. Which comes first, the chicken or egg?
2. Horses are such graceful animals.
3. God is king. He controls everything.
4. What is the vitamin that strengthens your bones?
5. Is a tomato a vegetable or fruit?
6. Wigs are convenient but could create a terrible mismatch.
7. Can you tell me of a fish recipe?
8. Why hasn't the meeting started?
9. I kept this seat warm just for you.
10. I am so happy to see a beauty like you!

TRANSFORMATION

As the heavenly light shines through you
Life-changing practices you'll soon develop
Happiness will reflect from your determined eyes
To be received by many on your roads of travel
Let your kindness be as piercing like a penetrating sword
Your kindness will be digested in the stomach of many
To be nourished by the practices which you developed
And strong they will become
In the belief that kindness is better
Gone forever are the choices they once cherished
In the garden of their minds, a new crop will be planted
And the fruits of kindness can be grown to be eaten
By the mouths of those who choose to listen.

CONVERSATIONAL TRIGGERS

1. Can you imagine life without law and order in this society?
2. Some of our preachers are becoming so tainted!
3. How often do you eat fish?
4. On what website can I order event tickets?
5. Some things will never change.
6. It's a shame that kindness is becoming obsolete.
7. Do you like sleeveless blouses?
8. We are displacing so many animals. Where can they go?
9. The master of deception will be on TV tonight.
10. Is the sound of church bells a thing of the past?

WOMAN IN PANTS

With the smile of a queen and the heart of a king
Into this world, from the cradle of your womb I came
From the elements of life, I was protected by your blanket of love
As I led my life through the valleys and mountains high
With rolled-up sleeves you lifted and freed me from falling rocks
The queen in you delighted my nurturing needs
By the king that's within were my roads of travel paved
The torch of guidance was lit by the glow of your loving eyes
Like a rushing river, into my ears your words of inspiration flow
With the smile of a queen and the heart of a king
Never did it seem that much was missing
Oh! My special mom! The love to you I'll never stop giving.

CONVERSATIONAL TRIGGERS

1. Do you feel very connected when you pray?
2. Is the Internet the highway of communication?
3. That skirt is a perfect fit!
4. Which do you like best, old or new Christmas songs?
5. I really love that color. It's my favorite.
6. Would you like to run in a marathon?
7. How well are you doing in school?
8. Tell me a good joke and cheer me up.
9. Have you recently moved to the neighborhood?
10. Did you see the super bowl?

FILTERED TONGUE

Destined to escape are the words of an open mouth
Speak, if you may but watch what you say
To others, it has been given when spoken
Like the wind, it will be acted upon by the listening ear
To be twisted and bent, may the revealed truth be destined!
With a new meaning, the contents may now be spoken
Speak, if you may, but watch what you say
Sound your trumpet with a rhythmic tune of caution!
Be not a prisoner in a jail of unspoken words
Like a key, the tongue must unlock the door of inner thoughts
As a steady stream of water, your words of thought will now flow
But remember, spoken words are not just for today
Speak, if you may, but watch what you say.

CONVERSATIONAL TRIGGERS

1. Who is the manufacturer of those tires?
2. Some people will never change.
3. Have you ever seen the Harlem Globetrotters?
4. Who is your favorite musician?
5. Do you repair TVs?
6. Refresh my memory! How many cards are in a deck?
7. I hate a tight-fitting shoe.
8. How long have you been working here?
9. Is the game finished?
10. You have a nice shape for jeans.

MAKING YOU WHOLE

Oh my precious but shattered princess!
I'll thread my needle with strands of love
And mend together the pieces of your broken heart
In the process of making you whole
I'll commence with magical hands
The stitches will be of precise spacing
To the hypnotic tone of my voice, you'll drift into a pleasant sleep
The tranquilizing stroke of my fingertips will free you of pain
By my body's boiling temperature, you'll be cleansed
With my scalpel of concern, I'll separate the splinters from your flesh
Now let the process of healing begin and be not afraid to love gain
And if by chance you have someone in mind, please let it be me.

CONVERSATIONAL TRIGGERS

1. Do you like your water very cold?
2. How do you rate the super bowl commercials?
3. Is the parade over?
4. Who is your favorite comedian?
5. Do you remember who did the first moonwalk?
6. Did you play dollhouse as a child?
7. What aspects of driving do you consider most difficult?
8. Have you ever collected baseball cards?
9. Do you look into the car next to you at a stoplight?
10. Those pearls are gorgeous!

MOST NATURAL

Listen to the tune that the wind sings
And reflect on the beauty that nature brings
Savor the sight of the dancing trees in the flowing wind
The mountains and hills are like castle walls that surrounds
A moisture-filled gray, the color of clouds will become
With advance notice, water will stream from the open sky
And water-filled bodies move like creatures on land
The light of nature's ceiling reflects from beyond
Evidence of nature's work will evolve as planned
On center stage, the blossoms of nature will be displayed
And with the colors that were created, a picture can be painted
Into your ears the birds will sing praise for a new beginning
As you listen, the words of "thank you, nature," should be given.

CONVERSATIONAL TRIGGERS

1. Oh! That's a very powerful message on your T-shirt.
2. What is your favorite card game?
3. What is the purpose of the food pyramid?
4. What type of art do you like?
5. Do you like jazz music?
6. Do you drink energy drinks?
7. Isn't it amazing that so many people are becoming eco-friendly?
8. Why aren't rainbows as colorful as they used to be?
9. Do you get flu shots?
10. What type of milk do you use?

ADVANCEMENT

The sign of caution was written on your precious face
With the conspicuous color called apprehension
And you rolled my way like a broken wheel
With the forward motion of a fractured spin
To my heart you arrived at the pace of a wounded snail
And transformed to a vessel in my stream of flowing blood
With your tall mast and sails with bulging wind
Into the depth of my heart you were directed
Your rush to acceptance is now guarded
By the absence of caution
In an instant, the hatch to your love was opened
With the flicker of an eye I was welcomed in
To drink from the cup of love you once shielded
At the celebration for you
You'll receive your championship ring.

CONVERSATIONAL TRIGGERS

1. Did you play with marbles as a child?
2. Where do you prefer to eat breakfast?
3. What style of jazz music do you like?
4. Have you ever played a pinball machine?
5. Can you play pool?
6. What type of books do you enjoy reading?
7. Do you find the thesaurus to be a very valuable tool?
8. Here comes the sun!
9. Does it seem to you that Nashville is somewhat like Hollywood?
10. Are those bags too heavy?

JUST CRY

The comfort in the emotion of crying
Can be soothing and reassuring
Let the tiny drops flow as a hemorrhaging wound
Down the paths of your hilly cheeks
Carrying self-pity and emotional waste to the floor
Just cry for whatever the reason. Just cry!
Wet your cheeks with the moisture of grief
As the flood of tears dissipates
To the calm you'll become acquainted
To the inner you, you must say, "Cleansed at last!"
And never will the path of your falling tears be blocked
So that the road to acceptance you may follow
Just cry for whatever the reason. Just cry!

CONVERSATIONAL TRIGGERS

1. Can you play a musical instrument?
2. Who is your favorite playwright?
3. The moonlight on a peaceful lake is very soothing.
4. Does the movement of the ticking clock stimulate you?
5. What function is the left side of the brain used for?
6. What's your favorite restaurant for dinner?
7. Wasn't the super bowl half-time show spectacular?
8. Why is the IRS so powerful?
9. Who won the Daytona 500?
10. What is the safest area in a home during a tornado?

GRANDMA THE BEAUTIFUL

From your reservoir of life essentials
To my mom, love and wisdom were delivered
The time has changed, but your priceless value still remains
You're as sweet as an angel with blanket wings
Which was often used to cover my chilly skin
Away from the unimportant things I was directed
And shed of the insecurities that lies within
Your massive heart anchored my drifting ship
The calm of your presence is as soothing as a sleepy breeze
By you I was guided to my true beauty and found it within
Like a star I'll shine my light of love on Grandma forever!

CONVERSATIONAL TRIGGERS

1. What is the safest area in a home during a hurricane?
2. Can you play chess?
3. Why are judges so powerful?
4. What is the category of plants that comes back every year?
5. What's the title of a present best-selling book?
6. Did you see the solar eclipse?
7. What does the term *wallet wise* mean?
8. Do you know the easiest way to peel a banana?
9. Who flew the first airplane?
10. Is cheese really a meat substitute?

GROUNDED

Clip my wings and make me your king
Away from you, never I'll fly again
Slow me to the pace of a wheel that's almost still
Cover my throne with the soft fabric you call skin
Restrict my flight with your shield of choice
To the queen in you, I'll instill my trust
Precious one, for you I will do whatever I can
I'll be your beach as you play in my crystal sand
Footprints of love can be seen in the trampled sand
Which leads to the water by way of land
Ripples in waves will cease beneath your walking feet
In the water of glass sits the beauty of your body's mass
With you in your ocean of love I'll always swim.

CONVERSATIONAL TRIGGERS

1. Would you like to work from home?
2. What is a doctorate of philosophy?
3. She's so precious!
4. What is the number one killer in the US?
5. Is there a hidden purpose to mega churches?
6. Give me your opinion on a no-cash society.
7. Tell me what your favorite TV show is?
8. Do you celebrate Christmas?
9. Who won the space race?
10. What size engine does your car have?

THE DESERVING MIND

To what use must you put a compliment
If it's not given to whom it's due?
Gather your thoughts! Be generous and start acknowledging
Relinquish your right to what's not yours!
Think of the deserving mind and not of your withholding thoughts
To the receiving mind, the energy of accomplishment will be felt
Think not only of the one who has done it
But of what has been done
A compliment is a gratuity in the form of spoken words
And the gratifying words of "thank you" will be reciprocated
Be not apprehensive in letting them know "job well done"
Please! Communicate the joy of appreciation to someone
And you will contribute to their day of production.

CONVERSATIONAL TRIGGERS

1. Do you prefer cars or SUVs?
2. Why do consumers accumulate so much credit card debt?
3. Why did you choose to be a flight attendant?
4. Where were you during 9/11?
5. Where is the closest hospital?
6. Are your parents still alive?
7. In a job, do you prefer high wages or good benefits?
8. Where is the next Olympic Game being held?
9. What do you think would be an alternative to gas?
10. On a man, do you like a full suit or jacket and pants?

DISGUISE

I met you at a very tender age
Not knowing I would end up caged
The fun you generated was extraordinary
The heights you took me to were where I wanted to be
All along I didn't know you were masking me
I was so involved with you I couldn't see
You used to make me feel so special
All along I didn't know you were a rascal
We've done so many things together
I swore at times, you were my lover
So I can't understand why you made me suffer
Is it because I wasn't that clever?
I wish I had been a little tougher
Even when spoken to, you never said a word
To my way of thinking I view that as absurd
You stand patiently for periods of time
It's up to me to keep you as mine
To your attention I must bring
You're not the person you pretended to be
But I must say you'll always get respect from me
And in return I hope you'll set me free
With those few words, I've just said good-bye to thee!

CONVERSATIONAL TRIGGERS

1. What are some of the symptoms of iron deficiency?
2. At which national park did the stunt man try to jump?
3. What function is the right side of the brain used for?
4. He is precious to have as a son.
5. Was your makeup done by a makeup artist?
6. Can you direct me to the nearest pharmacy?
7. What is the first national park in the US?
8. What TV network do you find to be more reliable?
9. Is it true that oatmeal is very high in fiber?
10. Why are some mail trucks driven from the right side?